Habit

The Top 100 Best Habits
How to Make a Positive Habit
Permanent And How To Break Bad
Habits

By Ace McCloud
Copyright © 2014

Disclaimer

Table of Contents

DEDICATED TO THOSE WHO ARE PLAYING THE GAME OF LIFE TO

WIN

KEEP ON PUSHING AND NEVER GIVE UP!

Ace McCloud

Be sure to check out my website for all my Books and Audio books.

www.AcesEbooks.com

Introduction

I want to thank you and congratulate you for buying the book, "Habit: The Top 100 Best Habits- How to Make a Positive Habit Permanent and How to Break Bad Habits."

Habits: We all have them. Whether you are an athlete or a scholar, an entrepreneur or corporate employee, a parent or a child, you have habits. If you find yourself giving in to others too easily, that's a habit. If you find yourself with an erratic sleeping pattern, that's a habit. Even if you complain too much or don't pick up after yourself, or if you have several bank accounts into which you deposit and manage your money, those are all habits. Drinking is a habit. Smoking is a habit. Even checking your email is a habit. The list of possible habits is endless.

Although your personal, day-to-day habits can seem insignificant and unimportant, they actually can play a huge role in your present life and future. One of the problems in the world today is that too many people are preoccupied with the "big picture," like figuring out what kind of career path to take, instead of focusing on "the little things," which can have a direct impact on the big picture.

For example, say you are a person who has eaten candy for breakfast ever since you were a child. You have done it for so long that it has become a habit once you have reached adulthood. As an adult, you obviously have to find a job so that you can live independently. Say you finally get your dream job, but you're so used to eating candy for breakfast that it affects your ability to stay energized and mentally sharp throughout the workday. Then what do you think will happen? Your work could decline, your ability to meet your goals could suffer, and you could ultimately be fired and be back at square one. When it comes down to it, if you had gotten into the habit of eating a healthy breakfast sooner, you could have excelled at your dream job, and you could have potentially lived an amazing life. Think about that example and see if you can think of any times in your life where something like that has happened to you.

There are two categories of habits: bad habits and good habits. Developing good habits versus developing bad habits is important because your brain executes your habits automatically. In other words, you don't have to *think* about doing something—you just do it, because your brain is so used to doing it. That can ultimately affect the outcome of your life. For example, not picking up after yourself is a bad habit (because your garbage will pile up) and washing your hands after using the bathroom is a good habit (because you will be consistently killing germs and limit your chances of getting sick). Your habits, both good and bad, ultimately help shape the kind of life you have.

We all have bad habits and we all have good habits. The key to living successfully is to try to develop more good habits than bad. Many people are afraid of change, but the good news is that habits are actually very easy to change. All it takes is a little bit of willpower and determination and a little bit of learning, all of which this book aims to provide. Six different categories of habits affect some of the most important areas of your life: physical health habits, mental health habits, work productivity habits, home productivity habits, financial habits, and eating habits. By breaking your habits down into these six categories, you can easily determine which ones you need to work on, so that you can quickly and easily improve your life. By focusing your energy on only the habits that you need to change, you can increase your chances of living a happy, fulfilling, and successful life.

This book contains some of the best habits that you can use to shape your life. First and foremost, you will learn how to develop strategies to learn new habits and unlearn bad habits easily. Then, you will read about some of the best habits in the categories of physical health, mental health, home and work productivity, finances, and diet. You will also learn how your choices can affect your habits and, ultimately, the outcome of your life. This book's discussion of habits is intended to help make your life happier and easier by teaching you how to implement the power of good habits into your life.

Chapter 1: How Habits Can Change Your Life

When many people hear the word "habit," they immediately think about bad habits—when a child sucks his thumb or when a person drinks too much or when a person oversleeps too often. Habits are associated with negativity so much that the word almost has a stigma. However, many habits are good, and when learned, they can potentially make your life better. Good habits are what drive positivity, success, and happiness. The key is to know what kind of habits to develop and what kind to leave behind. Habits can make or break your goals, so it is important to learn about the best ones.

The most important question to ask yourself when thinking about your life, your goals, and your habits is, "What do I want to achieve?" For example, if you want to live in Italy one day, one of your most important goals is likely to learn Italian. How do you begin learning the Italian language? You would make it a *habit* to study Italian for several hours per week. That brings you to the topic of *how* to form that into a habit. Habits are learned and everybody learns differently. Use the strategies listed below and experiment a bit with yourself to see what works best. Once you have a great strategy for learning new habits, you can begin thinking about your life, your goals, and the habits that you want to learn in order to get you where you want to be in life.

Best Habit-Forming Strategies

Stay Consistent. Consistency is key when trying to learn a new habit. If you do not practice it every day, or at least a few times a week, you risk the chance of not learning the habit. For example, if you want to make it a habit to brush your teeth every morning when you wake up, it will not become a habit if you only do it whenever you feel like it. You must use some willpower and determination to get up every morning and make yourself head straight to the sink. By doing it every morning, you will soon begin to do it on "autopilot."

Write About It. When you write something down, you are more likely to remember it or at least keep it in the back of your mind. By writing down your goal to learn a habit or habits, it can be easier to remember to pursue the change actively. Also, you can always refer to your notes when you are feeling tempted to give up. A good idea is to keep a habit-forming journal. You can write about your progress and your thoughts on forming new habits, which can be very inspirational. If you don't want to make a journal, at the very least have your goals written down on a piece of paper, and then try and review those goals daily.

Visualize. Visualization is a powerful habit-forming technique. If you have ever read about goal-setting, you have probably heard the advice to visualize yourself achieving your goals. Learning a habit is no different, because it *is* a goal. By thinking about what your life will be like once you've learned a new habit, you can feel more inspired and excited to reach the end. Since visualization is such a powerful and important strategy, check out this YouTube video, How to visualize your goals by Howdini, to learn more. Another good strategy to use when visualizing, is to visualize yourself or the scenario in the 3rd person. So try and pretend like you are observing yourself accomplishing a particular goal or doing the desired task from a distance away from yourself. Studies have shown that this increases the power of your visualization. While it is important to visualize the desired result, doing this too much can actually be a bit demotivating, as it tricks your brain into thinking the goal has already been achieved. So be sure to also visualize yourself doing the necessary steps in order to achieve your desired goal. For example, if your goal is to win a local race, besides visualizing yourself crossing the finish line in first, be sure to visualize yourself from a distance away running every day, training every day, eating healthy, and whatever other things you may deem necessary in order to achieve this goal.

Pick a Role Model. Sometimes, it is not easy to make a change in your life on your own. People often become easily discouraged or think that they cannot do it. One good way to stay focused is to pick a role model. Your role model does not have to be a person who has successfully learned the same habit you're trying to learn but he or she can be someone who has overcome obstacles in order to achieve success. For example, the builder of the Brooklyn Bridge was told he could never do it and he even got injured on the job. However, he still built the bridge and it stands today. Since his story is inspirational, it can serve as a message as to say, "Don't give up!"

Eliminate Temptations. To learn a new habit better, get rid of anything that will stop you from achieving your goal. As you probably know, it is very easy to give into temptation. You may give in with the mindset of, "it's only this one time," but many people lose track of how many times they give into temptation and it ends up negatively affecting their progress. So, when trying to learn a new habit, see if there is any way to eliminate the temptations in your life. For example, if you're trying to form a habit of eating better, don't keep junk food in your house.

Substitute an Activity. If you are trying to break a bad habit, it can be easier to replace that habit with a new one. For example, if you're trying to quit smoking but you're used to smoking while you watch TV, find something else to do as you watch TV. You could chew gum, drink water, massage yourself, or otherwise find a way to distract yourself. This way, your mind will not be clouded with the thoughts of smoking.

Develop a Trigger. If you've ever taken a basic psychology class, you've probably heard of triggers before. A trigger sends a signal to your brain, telling it to do something. You can create a trigger to help you stick to learning a new habit. For example, if you want to stop biting your nails, clap your hands together whenever you feel the urge to bite your nails. When you clap your hands and refrain from biting your nails, your brain will eventually learn to associate clapping with no nail biting.

Do it With a Friend. Similar to picking a role model, if you have a friend who wants to learn the same new habit or kick the same bad habit, do it together. Doing things with friends is always fun and easier. It also gives you both the opportunity to motivate each other towards success.

Use Reminders. Sometimes your life may get so busy and hectic that all you need is a reminder to help you learn a new habit. In this day and age, setting reminders is easy. You can use post-it notes, set an alarm on your cell phone with a memo, or keep a planner. One good technique is to align your reminders with places or times where you would need to practice your new habit the most. For example, if you're giving up junk food, it would make sense to keep a note on your fridge reminding you that you're trying to eat more fruits and vegetables.

Don't Give Up. One of the most important techniques is to never give up. It's easy to say "forget it," and give up on trying to learn a new habit altogether. However, as long as you practice most of the other strategies, it will be harder to give up because you've invested so much time and effort. Again, visualize the end results and think about how much better your life will be once you've successfully learned the new habit.

Start Small. One of the biggest mistakes that people can make when trying to learn a new habit is that they try to make too big of a change at the beginning or they make too many changes at once. Starting out big or overwhelmed will not get you anywhere and will more than likely stress you out to the point where you'll just say, "Forget it." The key is to start small and take one step at a time. For example, say you wanted to change your eating habits, your thinking habits, and your spending habits. Instead of trying to change all three at once, pick one and work with it until you're where you want to be. Then, pick another one, do the same, and so on.

Reward Yourself. Finally, do not be afraid to reward yourself for successfully learning a new habit! By rewarding yourself, you can give yourself something nice for all the hard work and effort you put into learning the new habit—you deserve it because chances are it wasn't easy! Knowing that you will get a reward at the end also gives you something to look forward to, therefore adding to your motivation.

How Long Does It Take?

Depending on the way you learn, not all of these habit-learning strategies will work for you. Once you have decided which of these strategies you would like to use, try them for a while, and then ask yourself another important question: "How is this strategy working for me?"

Again, there is no concrete answer as to how long you should spend trying to learn a habit or habit-developing strategy. Some people claim that you can learn a habit within 21 days. Others claim it takes a month and a few more claim that it can take a month and a half. To get the best results, you should spend as much or as little time as you need learning how to master habit-learning strategies and habits themselves. However, a good way to control your time is to occasionally pause and ask yourself, "How is this working out for me?" If it's working out for you—great! Keep going and continue to get the great rewards from your good habit. If it isn't working out for you or if you're not feeling any good progress, then go back to the list and try another strategy until you find one that fits for you.

Once you've figured out the best ways that you can learn a habit, the next step is to learn some of the best possible habits to have!

Chapter 2: The Top 100 Best Habits

This chapter will break the 100 best habits down into six categories. Each habit listed in this chapter is intended to help you improve an important area of your life.

Physical Health Habits

Having good physical health is the key to a happy and successful life. The way you take care of your physical health can determine how long you live, how likely you are to develop a disease, how much energy you will have, how healthy you are, and much more. Unfortunately, there are many people who do not pay much attention to their physical health. It's a good idea to try and learn several habits that you aren't currently utilizing to keep your physical health in good shape.

1) **Sleep Right.** Getting into good sleeping habits can have tremendous benefits on both your physical *and* your mental health. Your body can suffer many consequences without the proper amounts of sleep. Not getting enough sleep often leads to long, sluggish days, fatigue, mental dullness, and lowered productivity in both the workplace and at home. The most effective sleeping habit is to have a consistent sleeping schedule. By going to bed and waking up at the same time, your body and biological clock have a better chance to regulate. Another good way to ensure that you can sleep better is to make sure you sleep in a dark area and on a comfortable bed.

2) **Take Care of Your Oral Health.** Brushing your teeth twice a day may seem like a little, unimportant task, but the way you take care of your oral health can actually impact your overall health! Dentists recommend brushing your teeth for two minutes in the morning and two minutes before you go to bed. Spending four minutes a day brushing your teeth can save you hundreds or thousands of dollars in major dental care. What could have been a small cavity can quickly escalate into a root canal if you don't take care of your teeth. Another incentive is that your teeth will feel good and your breath will smell great!

3) **Take Care of Your Skin.** By getting into the habit of taking care of your skin, you can reduce your chances of looking old as you age. There are many ways to do this. A good body lotion is a good choice and aloe vera gel works wonders on the skin. You can also use a good moisturizing facial wash to stay looking healthy and young. For many more details on how to care for your skin and avoid aging, be sure to check out my book Anti-Aging Cure.

4) **Take Care of Your Heart.** Developing the habit of taking care of your heart and your cardiovascular health can greatly increase your chances of living a longer and healthier life. To get into this habit, you have to think about your diet. You could start by replacing fried food with heart-friendly

foods. Fruits and vegetables are always a good choice. You can also get into the habit of exercising, which is a great habit we will discuss in a bit. For more details on how to get into the habit of taking great care of your heart, be sure to check out my book Heart Disease Cure.

5) **Schedule Yearly Check-Ups**. By scheduling yearly check-ups with your doctor, you can increase your chances of being healthier and living longer. By going to your doctor each year, he or she can help you monitor any physical or mental changes in your body, or even catch something before it turns into a much bigger problem. If you ignore your body for too long, you may come down with a sickness that will be harder or impossible to shake. If you can get into this habit, you can also set a good example for your friends and family.

6) **Exercise.** Exercising your body is one of the best habits ever. As you probably know, exercising is a great way to look and feel excellent. It can help increase your longevity and it can fend off stress. To get into the habit of exercising, you can start off small. For example, start by taking a walk through your neighborhood and gradually work your way up to learning strength exercises. By getting into this habit, you can increase your chances of feeling energetic, productive, and motivated. Many of the world's top performers have exercise as one of their primary habits.

7) **Wear Protective Equipment.** A great habit that not many people do is to wear protective equipment when working out or performing an intense activity. For example, if you wear protective braces or wraps while exercising, you can limit your chances of damaging your body. If you wear a helmet, knee pads, and elbow pads when you go rollerblading, you can limit your chances of incurring a serious injury if you fall. People who put too much strain or wear and tear on their bodies tend to have higher chances of developing weak bones as they age. By protecting your body parts, you can heighten your chances of having stronger bones and skin as you age.

8) **Bring Pets and Kids on Exercise Trips.** Exercising is a great habit but it is also a great habit to include your pets and family when you go out to exercise. By taking your dog on a walk with you or taking a run with your kids, you will be benefiting others and you can also enjoy each other's company, which is good for strengthening your mental health and sense of wellbeing. It's also a great way to make fun memories.

9) **Eat a Balanced Diet.** Along with exercise, the habit of eating a balanced diet is a must. Getting into this habit may take time, since many people who eat badly are used to their current diet. However, by making sure that you get the recommended amount of each food group, you can increase your chances of living longer and building resistance against injuries. One idea is to start by making small changes (like wheat bread for white bread) and then gradually work your way up to learning healthy recipes. A great place to start is in my other book, Vegetarian Diet, Recipes, and Cooking.

It's also a great idea to eat 4-5 smaller meals throughout the day instead of three larger meals.

10) **Take Your Vitamins and Minerals.** If you don't already eat right or you're working toward it, you can get into the habit of taking vitamin and mineral supplements to help balance the level of nutrients in your body. The easiest way to do this is to take a one-a-day multivitamin, which contains most of the nutrients that your body needs. There are different kinds for men, women, and kids. To get into the habit of taking a multivitamin, you can take it with your breakfast so you get it out of the way first thing in the morning. Two multivitamins that I highly recommend are the Optimum Nutrition Opti-Men Multivitamin and Optimum Nutrition Opti-Women Multivitamin.

11) **Park Far Away.** Getting into the habit of parking far away is related to the habit of exercising. However, if you live a busy life or have a hectic schedule, it can sometimes be hard to find the time to work out. One way you can get around that obstacle is to park your car far away when you're driving to work, the store, a friend's house, or anywhere. Instead of trying to find the closest parking spot, try parking a block or two away. This way, you can get in some walking to and from your destination. It is a very easy and productive strategy.

12) **Avoid smoking.** If you're a habitual smoker, one of the best habits you can get into is to stop smoking! Smoking does not benefit your life in any way. From affecting your lungs to your heart to your skin to your overall body, smoking is something that you should completely avoid and/or eliminate from your life. However, as you are probably aware, tobacco is an addictive substance and it is not easy to just up and quit. To learn how to avoid smoking, please check out my book Quit Smoking Now: Quickly and Easily.

Avoid Drugs Completely. Illegal drugs like cocaine, heroin, ecstasy, crack, and others also have no benefits for your health. In fact, many of them negatively affect your brain and other important organs. They're also addicting and can cause you to lose too much weight, have irregular heartbeats, overheat, or lose brain cells. Even legal drugs, such as Xanax, Percocet or Vicodin, can be dangerous if not taken correctly. One of the best habits to get into is to avoid drugs altogether. Don't even reason to yourself that you'll just "try it" once because many of them can get you hooked on the first try. Some of the negative effects of addiction include a hard time getting or keeping a job, losing quality friends, and bad relationships with your family members.

13) **Drink Responsibly.** It is not a bad thing to drink alcohol socially or at a get-together, as long as you don't go overboard. Drinking alcohol in excess can lead to addiction, depression, lack of motivation and liver damage. On the bright side, drinking some types of alcohol in moderation, such as red wine, can be good for your body. Experts even say that a standard glass of red wine per day (1 glass for women, 2 glasses for men)

can help fend off heart disease. But if you don't want to drink, a baby aspirin taken once a day at night has similar good effects.

14) **Stretch.** Stretching in the morning and at night can help make your muscles more flexible and durable. It can help prevent injuries and sprains. Get into the habit of stretching each day, even if you're not planning to exercise. Taking a few minutes to stretch can reduce your chances of facing costly medical bills if you do have any accidents and it can help make you feel great as well. This is something I do every day and cannot recommend it enough! If you don't currently stretch, this is something you may want to seriously consider adding to your list of new habits.

15) **Play a Sport.** Playing a sport or joining a recreational sports team can bring many benefits to your life. It can be fun, it can encourage socialization, and it serves as a form of exercise. To help make this habit stick, join a team that meets a few times a week, so you get used to playing.

Your overall physical health is extremely important. If you want more advanced information on keeping yourself in top physical condition, be sure to check out my book: Ultimate Health Secrets.

Mental Health and Personal Growth Habits

In addition to your physical health, your mental health is also one of the most important things in your life. Having a clear and relaxed mind is essential for focusing, learning, and feeling happy. However, many people often find themselves stressed out by work, school, drama, relationship problems, and financial problems. The good news is that you can learn some great habits to help keep your mind healthy and balanced. With a strong mind, you can begin to learn habits that can assist you in your personal growth, which can lead to a successful career and all sorts of other opportunities.

1) **Think of Yourself before Others.** More likely than not, you have probably been in a situation where you've sacrificed yourself or your well-being for that of another person. If this sounds like you, a good habit that you may consider forming is to learn how to put yourself ahead of others. There are some situations where you *should* put others ahead of yourself, but in small, not dire situations, be sure to put your own feelings ahead of others. By taking care of yourself first, you should have more energy to help others when needed.

2) **Spend Time Outside.** Some people thrive and get energized from the outdoors. Some people even suffer from Seasonal Affective Disorder (SAD), which means that they actually fall into a depression when they spend too much time indoors, especially in the winter. Whether you suffer from SAD or not, a good habit is to spend a good amount of your time outdoors. Fresh air helps many people clear their minds and relax. Many people who expose their skin to sunlight also tend to have healthier skin,

because the sunlight provides your body with vitamin D. A daily walk is one of the best ways to get some good quality outdoor time in.

3) **Remember to Laugh.** Some people believe that the best type of medicine is laughter. Laughter is a well-known stress-relieving technique. Think about the last time you shared a funny moment with your family or exchanged a joke with a friend. Chances are that you felt happy and joyful in that moment. If you tend to be a serious and uptight person, you may sometimes forget to have a laugh and your stress levels could be higher than necessary. Remembering to laugh is an easy habit to get into. You can get your laughs in by downloading a jokes app to your phone, tuning into the Comedy Channel on your TV, buying a humorous book, or by spending time with others who love to laugh. For more ideas on how to fill your life with more laughter and job, please check out my book Laughter and Humor Therapy.

4) **Ask For Help.** Asking others for help when you need it is a great habit. Often, people get caught up in having too much pride and are afraid to ask others for help when they truly need it. For example, some people can be stubborn and refuse to let anyone help them lift a couch or some people may be embarrassed to ask for help with a project out of fear that it will make them look stupid. The truth is that asking for help will not make you look stupid or weak, and people are often more than happy to help each other. If you do not learn how to ask for help, you risk having your workload pile up and/or facing more stress in your life. If it comes to something like asking for help to lift something heavy, you run the risk of hurting yourself. Being helpful is human nature, so if you tend to try and do everything by yourself, you may want to try making this more of a habit.

5) **Practice Spirituality.** To be spiritual, you don't exactly have to be religious, but it can help ease any mental fog or stress that you may have. Spirituality is a mixture of willpower, motivation, and mental growth, under the mindset that everyone is loved. Being spiritual can help you differentiate between the times that you spend doing practical things, like working, paying bills, and exercising, from the small and enjoyable things in life that cannot be bought, such as taking the time to watch the sunset. Spirituality can help you remember to relax and enjoy life for what it is.

6) **Exercise Your Brain.** Just as you exercise your body, you must exercise your brain. If you do not use your brain regularly, you risk the chances of losing your mental sharpness. It is easier for children and teenagers to keep their brains sharp because they are required to do schoolwork and their peers are sure to keep them on their toes. However, some adults graduate school and then never make much of an effort to learn or push their boundaries. By exercising your brain regularly, you can improve your memory, your problem-solving skills and your overall mental sharpness. You can even get your brain to think more quickly. Sudoku

puzzles, crossword puzzles, reading, video games, board games and word puzzles are good tools for exercising your brain.

7) **Be Optimistic.** Have you ever heard that attitude is everything? People who have negative attitudes tend to be followed by negative actions and consequences. People who have optimistic and positive attitudes are more likely to realize their dreams and success. By simply having a positive outlook on life, your chances of living a fulfilling life can increase. For example, say that your friend worked a high-paying job and you worked a minimum wage job. If you constantly mope and wallow over the fact that your friend makes more money than you, you will be too busy and distracted from figuring out how to improve your own paycheck. Studies have shown that optimistic people have a much higher chance of spotting opportunities and capitalizing on them than pessimistic people.

8) **Develop Relationships.** Being close with others and knowing that you are surrounded by people who you can laugh, talk, confide, and just hang out with feels great. Sometimes being alone is good for relaxing, reflecting, and collecting your thoughts. However, being alone all the time can get lonely and frustrating. If you begin to develop relationships with the people you see every day, your social life can prosper and you will be generally be a happier person.

9) **Give More Hugs.** Almost nothing is comparable to the human touch. It is naturally comforting and relaxing. Hugs are a great way to remind your loved ones that you love and appreciate them. Hugging your loved ones and friends is a great habit to form and comes in handy when you know somebody could benefit from a hug! Also, the more hugs you give, the more hugs you are likely to receive. Giving other people hugs can also make you feel good about yourself.

10) **Reward Yourself.** Sometimes people get so caught up in trying to improve their lives that they forget to enjoy themselves and have fun. As you continue to improve upon your life and your lifestyle, don't forget to reward yourself for all the hard work! Rewarding yourself with a trip to your local amusement park or a new outfit can be very exciting and refreshing. It also helps you remember that hard work always pays off.

11) **Take Deep Breaths.** Believe it or not, some people forget to breathe, especially in nerve-wracking situations. The habit of taking deep breaths can have a positive impact on your mental and physical health. Deep breaths only take a few seconds and can help pump more oxygen to your heart and lungs. It can also serve as a way to put your life on pause and to relax for a few moments. You can take deep breaths at home, at work, or just about anywhere!

12) **Participate in a Soothing Hobby.** Having a soothing hobby, like knitting or reading, is a great habit. These types of activities usually take place in quiet areas, and allow you to relax your mind. They also help your brain to stay sharp because you're using it.

13) **Nap.** Napping is not just for preschoolers anymore. If you're an early riser or if you don't get a good night's sleep, taking a short nap during the day can help boost your energy levels and it allows your mind to shut down for a while. If you're not tired, try meditating or listening to a hypnosis soundtrack that is designed to help improve yourself in some way.

14) **Be Yourself.** Believe it or not, many people get so caught up in trying to be like other people that they forget to be themselves. For example, if you're trying to impress a person by dressing one way when you like to dress another way, you aren't being yourself. Changing your opinion to agree with someone else is another example. When you are yourself in the way that you dress, think, talk, act, and similar activities, it is usually much easier to be happy and relaxed. Also, many people are quite adept at knowing when someone is being fake, and that is quite a turn off. So in the majority of situations, it is best to just be yourself.

15) **Don't Gossip.** Gossiping is when you talk about another person's business or spread a piece of information, usually negative, about another person. Gossiping can be very contagious and entertaining but it can also be mentally draining and it can make you seem untrustworthy. A good habit is simply not to participate in any kind of gossip. Over time, avoiding gossip can save you energy, headaches, and improve your standing in many people's eyes.

16) **Don't Hold Grudges.** Holding grudges against others or even yourself can be mentally draining, especially if it is over something small and insignificant. It can hold you back from opportunities and it doesn't help anybody move forward in life. Learn to forgive others and yourself for a refreshed mind and spirit. While this is easily said, it can actually be quite difficult to do. In some cases, you will have to diligently work on this in order to free yourself from negative thoughts. For more help on this, be sure to check out the great "Tapping" videos on YouTube. Another good idea is to try out a forgiveness hypnosis sound track or for more techniques my Laughter and Humor Therapy book can help as well.

17) **Learn to Handle Rejection.** Having to deal with rejection is inevitable because at one point or another in your life, you will probably be turned down—whether you're rejected from a sports team, a college, a position, or anything else. Many people tend to let rejection discourage them, but if you can see it in a positive light, you can be much better off for the next opportunity. If you are rejected for something, view it as an opportunity to see what you can improve upon. Also, don't get all emotional if someone gives you criticism. They are usually just trying to help and if you can learn to take criticism without blowing your lid, then you will be much better off in your journey through life.

18) **Resist Fear.** Fear is a natural emotion, but many people allow it to control their lives. It is normal to be scared to take risks in your life but sometimes you can deny yourself a great opportunity if you don't try. Learning how to resist fear can open many potential doors for your future.

One great way to resist fear is to think about exactly what is holding you back and work on that specific fear. Even over a thousand years ago people knew that fortune favors the brave.

19) **Learn From Your Mistakes.** You can't learn unless you make mistakes. Many people allow their mistakes to discourage them but if you can view them as learning experiences, you will always gain personal growth. The key is to learn from your mistakes the first time. For example, if you neglect to brush your teeth and have to spend thousands of dollars on dental work, you should learn from that and begin to take better care of your teeth so it doesn't happen again. Even better than learning from your mistakes is to seek the advice of a mentor or read a good book on the subject you're currently interested in. Avoiding mistakes by taking the advice of others is the best route to take.

Work Productivity Habits

When you're at work, it is important to be productive, because more productivity equals more time, and more time equals more opportunities or money you can earn. To get the maximum productivity while you're working, some helpful habits can be developed.

1) **Take Breaks.** A great habit for improving your productivity at work is to take breaks. Some people like to stay working on a project until it is done, but when you focus on one thing for too long, your brain can tend to grow tired and unfocused. By taking a break, you can allow your mind to relax and refresh itself so that you can go back to your task and be able to fully focus.

2) **Practice Good Ergonomics.** If your job requires that you have to stay in a certain position for an extended period of time or move in a certain manner, you could end up with muscle injuries or disorders if you don't position your body correctly. There are certain ways that you can move or sit while protecting your body at the same time. For example, if you lift a lot at your job, you should get into the habit of bending at your knees and not your back. If you work at a desk all day, proper placement of your monitor, mouse, and keyboard are critical. If you do not practice good ergonomics, you can risk suffering an injury and your productivity may decline.

3) **Keep Your Workspace Clean and Organized.** If your workspace is cluttered or messy, your productivity levels can drastically decline. Important papers, ideas, or tasks can get swallowed in the clutter. A cluttered desk can also cause mental stress. It is important to get into the habit of keeping a clean and organized workspace. You can get into this habit by using desk organizing tools (like a paper holder or pen holder), organizational computer programs and you can throw away any food or drinks that you consume at your desk as soon as you're finished to keep it

clean. You may be surprised at how much better you feel when you have a crisp and clean workplace free from clutter and distractions.

4) **Monitor Your Workload.** To stay productive at work, it is a good idea to get into the habit of monitoring your workload. This is an especially good habit for the self-employed. For example, if you take on too many clients at once, you may become overwhelmed with work and get stressed out. However, if you are actively aware of your workload, you can have a better idea of when to schedule in more clients or work. This way, you can focus your energy on the optimum amount for the best results.

5) **To-Do Lists.** To-do lists may seem like a silly thing to do, but they can actually help you manage your day much more effectively. By getting into the habit of writing a to-do list each morning, you can have a better idea of how your day will flow. It can also help you organize and prioritize your tasks, which can help improve your productivity tremendously. My favorite thing to do is to cut up a bunch of small squares of paper and write down a goal or task on each one. I will then order them in priority in front of me on the desk, and throw them away once they have been completed.

6) **Prioritize Your Tasks.** By knowing which tasks on your to-do list are the most important, you can push the less important tasks to the end. When you take care of your most important tasks, you can work hard in the beginning and relax later.

7) **Love Your Job.** One great habit that many people overlook is to love their jobs. When you love your job, your motivation levels can go up and, as a result, so can your productivity. Even if you don't have a passion for what you do, try to think of one aspect of it that you really enjoy. Do you love being around your co-workers? Do you enjoy having your own office space? Do you enjoy the scenic route that you have to drive to get there? The possibilities are endless when it comes to finding something that you love about your job.

8) **Actively Participate.** Another work productivity habit that many people miss is the habit of actively participating. Some people just go to work with the mindset that they will just meet the minimum responsibilities and get paid. Those same people are the ones who find themselves wondering why they haven't received a raise or a promotion. If you actively participate, not only can you help the overall productivity level of your workplace improve, but you can also become a leader instead of a follower.

9) **Follow the 80/20 Rule.** The 80/20 rule is a well-known theory that suggests a great way for people to stay productive. The idea is that if you focus on the most important 20% of a task that produces the best results and mostly ignore the other 80%, then you will end up getting much better results. For example, if you're a baker and you notice that the majority of your sales come from fresh donuts, then it would be wise to focus the majority of your attention on making fresh donuts rather on other items that may not be selling well.

10) **Practice S.M.A.R.T.** Before you try to tackle a bunch of tasks at once, ask yourself if each one is specific, measurable, attainable, relevant, and timely (S.M.A.R.T). If the answer is "no," then you might want to put that task off until a later date. Getting into the habit of measuring your tasks with this acronym can save you a lot of time.

11) **Practice Goal-Setting.** Goal-setting is one of the most important habits to develop, especially if you're only going to establish a few "good" habits. You can set short-term and long-term goals to get where you want to be. Most likely, you will have many different kinds of goals in your life—diet goals, work goals, personal development goals, etc.

12) **Keep Idea Notebook.** If you're the type of person who is always coming up with ideas, it can be helpful to get into the habit of keeping an idea notebook. For example, you might come up with an idea for the world's next bestseller while you're at your day job—since you wouldn't be able to work on that idea in that very moment, you could pull out your notebook, write it down, and go back to it when you have time.

13) **Network.** Networking can be one of the most important things ever! Networking is becoming friendly with other people in your workplace, organization, or field. Many people end up getting great jobs and opportunities through networking. Networking works in several different ways. You could carry around your business cards, send people messages on LinkedIn, or just simply strike up a conversation with somebody with the hopes that they will remember you for a later opportunity. You may be surprised at just how many good things can happen when you meet the right people and work together for mutual benefit.

14) **Turn Off Social Media.** Social media, such as Facebook, Twitter, YouTube, and Google +, is great for networking and learning information, but it can also be very distracting. If you have access to the internet on your work computer, see if you can block yourself from accessing those websites. If you have social media apps on your phone, simply turn your phone off while you're working. You can always go back to social media during your free time.

15) **Say No.** If you are the kind of person who says yes to everything, you may find it hard to prioritize your most important tasks or to get things done. When you say no to something, nothing horrible will happen. You can always reschedule something later.

16) **Think Creatively.** By thinking outside of the box, you can really make yourself stand out to your boss and coworkers. Thinking creatively and differently allows you to implement new ideas in your workplace and it also shows people that you are good at finding solutions. If everybody else around you tends to look for easy solutions, show that you are different by thinking of something unique.

17) **Don't Complain.** It can be tempting to complain about your job or your responsibilities, but nothing good ever came from complaining. It doesn't

change your situation and if your boss or coworkers overhear you complaining about your job, it can tarnish your character and your chances for advancement. Complaining can also be mentally draining, so it is not even worth doing.

18) **Finish Anything You Start.** By finishing any projects that you start, you can show others that you're a hard-working, dedicated, and committed employee. Once you've finished what you've started, you can also feel good about yourself, knowing that you can accomplish things and follow through on the things that you say.

19) **Encourage Others to Succeed.** Many people tend to respect those who push others to succeed. It shows that you're not conceited, arrogant, or selfish. It also supports a sense of teaching and mentoring, which can always benefit people and help others improve upon themselves. In a world where many people tend to be selfish, encouraging others to succeed can be fulfilling and it could even help change the world.

Home Productivity and Health Habits

Home is the place where you can relax and enjoy yourself, but if you live by yourself or have children, it is important to know how to spend your time at home wisely. Luckily, there are many great habits that you can learn to make the most out of your time spent at home.

1) **Cook Your Own Meals.** In today's fast-paced world, it can be tempting to eat out at fast food restaurants or eat frozen dinners because they are fast, accessible, and easy. The main drawback is that most fast food restaurants and frozen dinner manufacturers use food of poor quality, and restaurants usually cook it in unhealthy oils, which can ultimately lead to health issues. By cooking your own meals, you will know exactly what you're eating and you can monitor how much healthy food that you and your family eat. Cooking can also be fun. There's no better feeling than taking a bite out of your first home-cooked meal and saying, "Wow, did I really make this?"

2) **Start a Garden.** Gardening is a great habit to get into because it has many benefits. Gardening can help your mind relax, it gets you outside, and it keeps you busy. You can even plant small vegetables that you can later eat in your home-cooked meals. If you have kids, you can let them help out in the garden, which can lead to spending quality time with them. Your kids can also learn about plants and gardening.

3) **Eat with Your Family.** Eating dinner with your family is a habit that has gradually declined over the last decade. It used to be a common practice but now that many households need two sources of income, more husbands and wives are going to work, and the 9 to 5 workday has also started to fade, so many families have conflicting work schedules, making it hard to spend time with each other. As a result, parents are becoming

out of tune with their kids' lives and families can quickly forget how good it is to spend quality time with each other. Even if you can only get together with your family once a week, it is a habit that is well worth the effort.

4) **Appreciate Your Family.** When you live with your family or see them almost every day, it can be very easy to take them for granted. Forgetting to appreciate your family can result in misunderstandings, hurt feelings, or other conflicts, so it is important to remember to do so. You can get into the habit of appreciating your family members by complimenting each other, helping each other out, or just by simply thanking them or saying that you love them.

5) **Make Organic Cleaning Supplies.** By making or using organic cleaning supplies, you can protect yourself and your family from chemicals. Do a favor for the environment, and protect the surfaces you clean. The benefits of making or using organic cleaning supplies far outweigh the cons. To get this habit started, check out this YouTube video posted by eHow, Gorgeously Green - How to Make Organic All-Purpose Cleaner, for more information.

6) **Plan Your Meals.** Planning your meals is a great habit because it can help you save money and time. It can also help you become more aware of what you and your family are eating. If you plan out everything that you are going to cook or make at the beginning of the week, you'll know what you need to buy from the store and you'll know approximately how much time you'll need to make it, thus making your life a bit more organized. You can also make extra large portions when cooking, and save them for later.

7) **Avoid the News Channel.** Watching the news can potentially suck the productivity right out of some people. While you should know what is going on in the world and in your community, keeping the news on in the background can be highly distracting. If you're a very sensitive person, you may see some stories on the news that can upset you and disrupt your day. One of the best ways to avoid watching the news channel is to read the newspaper in the morning to get all your information. If you're concerned about missing any breaking news, there are ways to get breaking news notifications sent to your smart phone and email accounts. However, most truly productive people get better results from focusing on more important things that matter to them rather than on the daily news.

8) **Clean as You Go.** Instead of waiting for your clothes to pile up on the floor or for your garbage can to overflow, clean as you go to save time and effort in your life. Get into the habit of taking out the trash as soon as you see it full or putting your clothes right into your hamper instead of on the floor. This way, you can keep your clutter to a minimum and you won't have to set aside certain days to clean everything all at once.

9) **Set Tomorrow Up, Tonight.** Setting up your next day on the night before can be an excellent habit. You could simply make a to-do list of

everything that needs to be done, whether at work or at home. You could lay your clothes out the night before, set up your breakfast food for easy preparation, stretch, or do anything else that can help you to prepare for the next day. This can save you time and energy to get other things done.

10) **Go through Your Things Every 6 Months.** If you tend to have a lot of clothes, toys, electronics, books, or anything, make it a habit to sort through your stuff every 6 months. This can help you decide what things you still need or want and what things you don't. Then you could donate your old things to the less fortunate, sell them, or give them away to family and friends. This can help you minimize clutter and make room in your house for new things that you may want.

11) **Spend Time With Family.** I touched on this a few habits earlier, but if you absolutely can't make a meal with your family, you can make it a habit to spend your time with them some other way. You can read to your children at night after work, you can have breakfast with your family; you can plan outings with them, or you can do anything that you can all schedule in together.

12) **File Your Bills and Important Paperwork.** Filing your bills and important paperwork, such as wills, birth certificates, contracts, receipts, or pay stubs can help you stay organized and you will always know where to find those documents when you need them. Filing your bills can also help you keep track of knowing where your money is going every month. Filing these papers can be as simple as keeping them in a shoebox or storing them in a filing cabinet.

13) **Do One Load of Laundry per Day.** If you or your family tends to let piles and piles of laundry build up until you don't have any clean clothes, you could start to do one load of laundry per day. By washing whatever is dirty each day and taking a few minutes to fold it and put it away, you can save yourself time and your home has a better chance of staying clean and organized.

14) **Make Time for Yourself.** Since your home is the best place to relax, be sure to schedule some time for yourself after you get all of your hard work done. In the midst of taking care of your work and home responsibilities, it can be easy to forget to take care of yourself. Set some time aside to do whatever you enjoy—whether it's watching TV, reading a magazine, taking a nap, or sitting in the sunlight. Spending some down time with yourself can also allow your mind and body to rest, letting it recharge for your next tasks.

Financial Habits

In today's economy, money can often seem tight or scarce, making it very valuable to those who have to front their own cost of living. A few good habits can help you master the art of spending and saving money.

1) **BYOB-Bring Your Own BAG.** When you go shopping, bring your own shopping bags and don't use a cart. This can help offset impulse buying because you'll have to carry anything that doesn't fit in your bags. Bringing your own bags is also good for the environment. For example, if you go to the grocery store knowing that you only need milk, bread, and eggs, just bring one bag so you don't absentmindedly fill an entire shopping cart with items that you don't need.

2) **Only Buy What You Need.** If you don't use your own bags when you go shopping, you should get into the habit of buying only what you absolutely need. This will take some willpower and determination but it is possible. It can help you save money and you won't end up spending more time in the store than you anticipated.

3) **Save Money on Bottled Water.** Instead of buying bottled water at the store, which can be very expensive in some places, you can get into the habit of filtering your own water and bottling it yourself. Not only will this have a positive impact on your wallet but it can help the environment, too. A really great product that you can use to filter tap water is the Zero Water Pitcher. I personally use this pitcher to filter my water and not only does it save me money, but the water tastes great.

4) **Consider Pre-Owned.** If you're looking to save money, you can consider buying pre-owned things as opposed to brand new. Most thrift stores have high quality, used clothing, furniture, books, and other household accessories that are almost as good as new. Many reputable car dealerships offer certified pre-owned cars that drive like new ones as well. Even the big video game stores sell pre-owned video games at a discounted price. Buying pre-owned items can save you a lot of money if done wisely.

5) **Plan Your Budget and Review Monthly.** One of the biggest mistakes that many people make when it comes to finances is that they don't plan a budget for themselves. If you are used to mindlessly spending your money, it can be easy to forget how much you spend every month. However, if you take the time to sit down and compare your salary to your monthly bills, you can figure out where to cut or increase your spending. A simple review can help save you hundreds of dollars each year. It is also good to get in the habit of reviewing your budget each month, because things change. Gas prices are constantly changing, your heating bill probably goes down in the summer and up in the winter, and even if you're a safe driver, your car insurance rate can change.

6) **Save a Little Each Month.** If possible, save whatever money you can each month, even if you only put $20 aside. That can save you $240 a year and you never know when you might need it, because cars break down, teeth get cavities, accidents happen, etc. There is no worse feeling than finding yourself in an emergency situation and without money.

7) **Practice and Develop Good Credit Skills.** Having a good credit score is important for various reasons—renting an apartment, buying a new car,

or buying a house. You can build your credit score by making loan payments or by paying your credit card bills on time. The earlier you establish credit, the better your credit will be as you age, since part of your credit score is based on how long you've been making payments on something.

8) **Share a Financial Goal with a Friend.** Since managing money can be very challenging at times, it can be helpful to keep track of your progress with a friend. I mentioned earlier how committing to learning a habit with a friend can be motivating, encouraging, and even fun. You can stop each other from impulse buying if you shop together or you can give each other ideas on how to save money.

9) **Keep Your Spending Organized.** If possible, try to allocate the average amount of money that you spend per month to each of your bills. For example, if you know that you have to pay $100 for your car insurance each month, be sure that you don't spend that money on something else. One good way to organize your spending is to use cash or one debit card for your daily needs and one bank account for your absolute needs.

10) **Use Two Wallets.** I actually learned this trick in college. One great money-saving habit is using two wallets. This way, you can carry the amount of cash that you know you'll need on you when you go shopping and you can leave the other wallet with all of your other credit and debit cards home. This way you won't be tempted to overspend. Also, if you ever find yourself the victim of a robbery, you can give the robber your wallet that doesn't contain all of your money and ID's. In most cases, the robber won't know the difference as long as he's gotten away with your wallet.

11) **Know Your Debit Cards**. If you have multiple checking accounts at the same bank, they will likely give you two debit cards that have the same design and just different account numbers. This can lead to confusion and if you swipe a debit card that doesn't have money on it, you could overdraw your account. When that happens, you usually have to pay a fee. Get into the habit of strictly keeping your debit cards separate, or alternatively, memorize the last four digits of each card so you reduce your chances of overdrawing.

12) **Carry Cash for Gas.** For those who need to drive a lot, spending money on gas is inevitable. With rising gas prices across the globe, spending money on gas can be a nightmare for some. By getting into the habit of carrying cash, you reduce the risk of being in a situation where you can't pay for a refill or other car emergency.

13) **Have a Night "In" Instead of "Out".** Instead of going out with your friends or spouse, plan a nice night in. Staying home and catching a movie free-on-demand with a bowl of microwave popcorn beats paying $20+ for movie theater tickets and snacks. Snacks at the movie theater concession stand tend to be terribly overpriced. As long as you bring along a good

attitude, you can have just as much fun staying home as you can going out. Your habit of going out will easily fade once you see how much fun you can have staying in.

14) **Don't Immediately Throw out Something Broken.** If your favorite pair of pants gets a tear or if your washing machine suddenly stops working, don't be quick to throw it away and get another. Sometimes, you can easily repair something that is ripped or broken for a small price. For example, replacing a plug in your washing machine can be much cheaper than flat-out buying a whole new machine.

15) **Be Smart about Your Utilities.** This habit is a little obvious but for some reason, people still leave their lights and heat on all day, even when they go out. When you're not using your lights, heat, or other utilities, it's kind of silly to have to pay for that time when you could be using the money on something else. If you are used to forgetting to turn off your lights and heat when you leave home, you could post a reminder to yourself by the front door.

16) **Buy Generic.** Instead of buying the brands that you normally would (for example, big brands such as Coke, Tide, Hostess, etc), give the generic brand a try. Sometimes, the store brand of a product can taste as good or work just as well as the name brand and it's almost always cheaper. You might be surprised to know that some name brand companies even produce their products under a private label. In other words, that store brand detergent could even be Tide. You can also save a lot of money by using generic medicines versus brand name medicines.

17) **Service Your Car Annually.** Like scheduling your yearly check-ups, getting into the habit of servicing your car once a year can end up saving you tons of money. Your mechanic can often identify any problems that your car may have before it blows your engine or transmission. Regular work, such as tune-ups and filling your tires, has also been known to save you on gas mileage.

18) **Buy in Bulk.** Some stores like Walmart or Costco allow you to buy products in bulk, which can be cheaper than buying them individually. The best way to get into this habit is to figure out what products you use the most and only buy those in bulk. Buying in bulk can also save you extra trips to the store.

Eating Habits

With a limited amount of time during the day and a wide array of food choices, it can be hard to practice the best eating habits. Bad eating habits can lead to health problems and a bad self-image. Luckily, there are some great strategies for practicing the best eating habits possible.

1) **Make Time for Breakfast.** Out of all the meals you have in a day, breakfast is the most important. It is the first thing that you put in your

body each morning, which can make all the difference in terms of your energy. If you do not eat breakfast and you dive straight into your day, your chances of feeling tired, weak, and sluggish by the afternoon can greatly increase. When you do get into the habit of eating breakfast, make sure it's a healthy one!

2) **Stay Hydrated with Water.** Staying hydrated is important because it helps your heart pump blood through your body and it can refresh your body during a hot or humid day. Water is also one of the best drinks because it has no calories.

3) **Eat More Small Meals.** Instead of eating three big meals each day, start eating more small meals. Eating more, but smaller, meals can help you stay full throughout the day and it can help offset snacking or overeating. You don't even have to spend time making different meals—you can split one meal in half and eat the other half later.

4) **Keep Junk Food Out of Fridge.** To avoid snacking and overeating in between meals, one good habit you can get into is to simply keep junk food out of your fridge. If you don't have it, you can't eat it. To avoid buying it as you shop, spend 10 seconds telling yourself why you don't need it every time you start to put it in your cart.

5) **Eat Healthy Snacks between Meals.** As an alternative to snacking on junk food, try healthy snacks. Get into the habit of keeping your fridge stocked with sliced fruit, vegetables, ranch dip, yogurt cups, bags of trail mix, etc.

6) **Eat Slowly.** The more slowly you eat, the more you can enjoy and appreciate your meal. It's also been proven that eating more slowly can help you lose weight, have better digestion, and even reduce stress.

7) **Eat Before You Go Food Shopping.** By getting into the habit of eating before you go food shopping, you can reduce your likeliness to overspend or buy food that you don't really need. If you walk into the grocery store and you're hungry, you will often have a craving for almost everything you see. However, if you go on a full stomach, you will have a better shot at just buying what you really need.

8) **Track Your Progress and Monitor Your Eating.** If you're trying to improve your eating habits, get into the habit of keeping track of your progress. If you're trying to lose weight, get into the habit of monitoring what you eat. That way, if you're losing weight you'll know what's working and if you're not, you can figure out another route to take.

9) **Treat Yourself.** If you commit to learning better eating habits, reward yourself with a treat—your favorite ice cream cone, a soda, or whatever you've cut out of your diet. When you're working on improving your eating habits, there's no need to cut junk food completely out of your diet. When you learn to have it only once in a while, you'll enjoy it more and your body will thank you.

10) **Learn New Recipes.** To avoid getting bored with planning and cooking your meals yourself, start keeping your eyes peeled for new recipes. Not only can it help you get creative in the kitchen but it can also encourage you to stick to healthy eating. Eating the same foods and dishes over and over again can quickly become bland. New recipes are always delicious and exciting.

11) **Don't Carry Snack Money.** If you have to go to work or school, don't make it a habit to carry money for snacks. Vending machines tend to be overpriced and they hardly ever contain healthy snacks. Also, if you don't carry snack money, you can reduce your chances of overeating. A better idea is to bring a healthy snack from home with you, if you tend to get hungry in between meals.

12) **Bring Your Own Lunch.** By bringing your own lunch to work, school, or on an outing, you can save money, eat healthier, and you'll know exactly what you're eating. Buying lunch out can get pretty costly. It takes time because you have to wait for it to be prepared, and you can never be too sure what you're putting in your body, especially if you're buying lunch from a fast food restaurant or cafeteria.

13) **Add Ice.** If you love to drink sugary drinks like soda or juice, you can add ice to it. Adding ice to it will take up more room in your glass, causing you to drink less. Since you should only drink sugary beverages in moderation, adding ice to your glass can allow you to treat your taste buds while ensuring that you don't drink too much.

14) **Utilize Leftovers.** If you make a meal and it's too big or you can't finish it, wrap it up, put it in the fridge or freezer, and have it the next day. Food costs money and money is a valuable resource, so if you throw away perfectly edible food, you're basically throwing away money. You can also get creative and reuse leftovers by turning them into a new dish.

Chapter 3: How to Break a Bad Habit

Now that you have an idea of some of the best habits you can learn for a happy and successful life, the next step is to learn how to eliminate your bad, negative habits to make room for the new, positive ones. The definition of bad habits varies. Some "bad" habits are clearly bad, such as smoking, drinking too much alcohol, doing drugs, and eating poorly. There is no question that those habits can have detrimental effects on your life. However, there are some habits considered to be "bad" but not life-threatening. For example, not cleaning your house, breaking promises, or talking loudly on your cell phone in a public area are all considered bad habits by many. Though they may seem to be minor, if you can think of how your life can be better without those bad habits, you should try to break free from them. This chapter aims to teach you all about unlearning bad habits.

Breaking free from bad habits may sound like a daunting task, especially since you're used to engaging in your bad habit on autopilot. The good news is that since habits are learned, they can be unlearned as well. And remember that even if you've tried to break free from a bad habit in the past but failed, it doesn't mean that you shouldn't try again.

The #1 thing you should do before delving into any bad-habit-breaking strategy is to prepare yourself for the change. Most often, people rush into a change without thinking of the obstacles and challenges that await them on the other side. By taking a minute to prepare yourself for what's ahead, you can already get one step further toward unlearning a habit. Remind yourself that nobody is perfect. There may be times where you will "slip up" or feel the urge to go back to your bad habit. Do not beat yourself up if you fall into temptation, because nobody is perfect!

Here are some excellent strategies that you can use to unlearn some of your worst habits:

Use Willpower Sparingly. Did you know that your amount of willpower is similar to your muscles? The more you use and exert it, the more quickly it will tire out and need to refuel. When preparing yourself to break a bad habit, don't try to make it happen all at once. Take it day-by-day, little-by-little. Each day, your willpower will refresh itself and you will be ready to put your all into kicking the habit.

Be Healthy in Advance. If you are trying to improve your general health and kick a bad habit at the same time, you may not be as successful. To have a better shot at breaking a bad habit, you should wait until your health is in the best possible shape. The healthier you are, physically and mentally, the better you will be able to focus on positively changing your habits. Being in good health means that you will feel more energized, motivated, and determined to make changes in your life.

Set a Time Frame. A great strategy to break a bad habit is to set a time frame. By choosing a "start" and "end" date, you can have a better sense of how long you have to break your habit and that can help you plan for the change accordingly. Many people prefer to use 21-day, 30-day, and 60-day periods. Personally, I think as long as you pick a start and end date, the time it takes to break the bad habit is up to you. Since everybody is different, it may take some people longer and others may need less time. When you've decided on your start date, begin to plan your strategy week-by-week. Set goals for yourself and work your way to the finish line.

Be Specific in Your Goals. One of the biggest mistakes that people make when trying to break a bad habit is that their goals are not specific enough. A specific goal with a detailed plan serves as a better guide than a vague goal with no certain details. For example, instead of saying, "I want to get out of the habit of eating junk food," say, "I will easily get out of the habit of eating foods that contain sugar, fat, additives, and preservatives and replace them with foods that contain fruits, vegetables, and whole grains." The "I will easily" part at the beginning makes a goal feel much more attainable.

Go Slow. Another big mistake that people commonly make when trying to break a bad habit is that they try to go "cold turkey," meaning that they try to stop all at once. This is especially true when trying to break free from an addictive substance, such as tobacco, alcohol, or even caffeine. Instead of having your "last" of an addictive substance or performing a habit for the "last" time, try to wean yourself off of it. For example, if you are trying to get out of the habit of drinking caffeine, gradually cut down how much of it you drink each day. If you're used to drinking 20 cups of coffee a week, limit yourself to 15 during Week 1 and then go down to 10 during week 2 and so on. Eventually, you should be able to make it down to only a few or no cups each week.

Use Different Rewards and Incentives. Rewarding yourself for learning a good habit or unlearning a bad habit can be effective, but if you keep rewarding yourself with the same thing, you risk the chance of becoming bored with your reward. If you reward yourself differently for each bad habit unlearned, or for achieving each step toward unlearning a bad habit, you may not become discouraged as fast. For example, instead of rewarding yourself with a movie night for each bad habit unlearned, give yourself one movie night, one trip to the ice cream store, one massage, etc.

Have Substitute Activities in Mind. If you're trying to get out of the habit of something such as playing video games or watching too much TV, a good strategy to kick the habit is to substitute the activity with something better. For example, you could try reading a book during your usual TV time or you could plan to hang out with your friends during the time you'd normally play video games. In both instances, you would be gaining either knowledge, reading skills or social skills.

Use Reminders (Again).   Reminders are great for both learning and unlearning habits. If you work during the day and then take care of your family at night, it can be very easy to let the smaller details slip your mind.

Keep Yourself Accountable. A great way to help yourself unlearn a bad habit is to make yourself accountable. For example, if you let your friends and family or even the general public know that you're committing to unlearning a habit, they will be counting on you to follow through. You can keep yourself accountable by announcing your decision on social media, sharing your decision at the dinner table, or even by just letting someone know that you're planning to do it. Knowing that people are counting on you to succeed can be very motivating.

Use Social Media to Your Advantage. Again, social media can be very helpful when it comes to unlearning a habit, as long as you're not trying to get out of the habit of spending too much time online! In addition to announcing your goal to your friends and followers, you could use social media for inspiration. There are many pages that share pictures of inspirational quotes that can encourage you. You can also join online support groups or post updates so that you can keep yourself accountable. Facebook pages, Pinterest, and Tumblr are the three best websites for inspirational quotes. YouTube is a great place to find "how-to" videos that may relate to the habit you're trying to unlearn. You can post your real-time progress updates on Twitter.

Tune Out Haters. One thing that often holds people back from achieving their goal of unlearning a habit is that they have no support from their family and friends. If you are surrounded by people who try to tell you that you will not be successful or who somehow discourage you from trying, you probably will not succeed. However, if you surround yourself with positive, supportive people, you stand a higher chance of succeeding. Thinking positive thoughts can be a very powerful tool, so be sure to check out this YouTube video Stop Negative Thinking! by Jonathan Parker on how to stop negative thoughts.

Turn to a Professional. Finally, if you are truly struggling with unlearning a bad habit, you might consider turning to professional help. If you've ever thought about trying hypnosis, Hypnosisdownloads.com has some great resources on breaking habits and some of them are even habit specific. Here are some good titles: Break bad habits, Stop picking your skin, Drink less wine, Thumb sucking, Impulse buying, Nail biting, stellar success, stop negative thoughts, and much more.

If your bad habit is related to drugs or alcohol, you may need to seek help from a rehab or detox facility to fully recover. Since such substances are addicting, your body will go through withdrawal if it does not receive the substance that it's used to getting. Withdrawal can often be serious and painful. Most people who suffer from withdrawal experience anxiety, throwing up, sleeplessness, paranoia, and sometimes even hallucinations. Professional drug help facilities often have doctors and nurses available to monitor you and help you get through that process. Substance abuse recovery sometimes requires therapy, as well. If your addiction is mild or if you've already gone through a detoxification process, you can consider joining a support group to help you uphold your commitment to being clean. Many local churches and organizations host free and anonymous support groups.

Another option for getting professional help is to see a therapist or psychologist. Therapists and psychologists can be helpful if you need to talk about your habit since they are great listeners. They also tend to be very knowledgeable and may be able to work with you to find a solution to unlearning your habit. Specifically, behavioral therapy can help you break many obsessive-compulsive habits, and it can help you improve your social skills and your emotions. If you think you can benefit from behavioral therapy, you can search the internet for behavioral therapists in your area.

Chapter 4: The Power of Keystone Habits and Choices

Just how powerful are habits? Even if you decide to learn one new habit, it can ultimately affect other areas of your life. For example, if you get into the habit of exercising, not only will you be improving your body but you'll be improving in many other aspects of your life. Exercise can help fend off mental stress, therefore causing you to become more energized, therefore causing you to become more productive at work, therefore causing you to make more money, and so on. Keystone habits suggest that once you spend time learning new, positive habits, you will begin to pick up other positive habits without even being aware of it.

Keystone Habits

Keystone habits create a chain reaction of events. For example, if you start exercising and you only do it for one week, you may not feel stress-free and energetic right away, but over time, you will most likely notice a change. How does this work?

First, keystone habits serve as their own incentives. When you learn a new positive habit and you view it as a "win" for yourself, your chances of wanting another win can increase. Eventually, your small wins may lead you to setting bigger and better goals for yourself. Second, as I showed in the example above, they can help you unconsciously pick up more good habits. Third, keystone habits can make you feel more energized and confident. Once you see that you've picked up a good habit that has positively changed your life, you may feel more compelled to pick up more positive habits.

If you can understand how keystone habits work, you can have better control on the outcome of your life. You can control your physical health, your mental health, your energy and productivity levels, your spending habits, and your eating habits. All of these categories make up the majority of the most important things in your life.

Choices

Before a behavior can become a habit, it starts off as a choice. You are not born with any habits—they form from the choices you make. When you choose to do something over and over again, it will eventually become a habit, whether good or bad. The key to forming good habits is to start as early as possible and to make the best decisions that you can. Of course, nobody is perfect and everybody will make mistakes from which they can learn. However, as long as you understand how to make good choices, your chances of having more good habits than bad can improve.

Good choices have no concrete formula, but you can experiment with some techniques in order to learn how you can make the best choices possible. Often, your decisions can be influenced by your environment, the company you keep, and your emotions. Knowing how to start trying to make good decisions can make a huge difference in your life. What are some good ways to start?

Listen to Your Gut. While you shouldn't let your instincts control you completely, it is often a good idea to at least listen to them. Can you think back to a time where you had a "gut" feeling about something and it turned out that you were right? When you are faced with making a choice, take a few moments to ask yourself what your reasoning is for making that choice. Question your thoughts and feelings before saying yes or no. Taking a few minutes to reflect on your instinct can make all the difference.

Review Your Alternative Choices. Before making a choice, be sure to think about all of your other options. If you have to make a choice about something and you have ample time to think it over, one good strategy is to list all of the routes you can take. Spend a few minutes on each option and ask yourself specific questions. This can help you gain a better sense of what choice is better for your life.

Reword the Question. This may seem redundant, but if you are faced with a choice, try rewording the question for different alternatives. When your brain can see a problem from a different angle, it is sometimes be easier to make a better decision.

Sleep On It. In life, you must make some choices on the spot, without any time to think. However, you shouldn't jump to make any choices if you don't have to give an immediate answer. By taking your time on making a choice, you can think about the consequences that will come with each route you could take.

Learn From Your Mistakes. To make better decisions in life, sometimes you have to make a poor decision first. Some people don't understand the consequences of their actions unless they've already found themselves in hot water. If you're faced with a choice and you've been in a similar situation before, think back to the mistakes you've made. If you've already made one poor choice, you should go for the better choice next time.

Remember, the choices you make can quickly turn into your habits. If you make poor choices, like the decision to do drugs, you will more than likely develop a drug habit, which can ruin your life. If you make good choices, like paying attention in school, you can get into the habit of being able to learn easily and work hard and you may stand a better chance of having a successful career. By knowing how to make the best choices possible, you can have a better grasp on controlling your life. Think about your choices and how keystone habits can turn your good choices into great habits. If you find yourself lacking in willpower or discipline, be sure to check out my bestselling book: <u>Self Discipline and Willpower</u>.

Conclusion

I hope this book was able to help you to learn the importance of good habits and how they can positively change your life.

The next step is to evaluate your own habits. Do you have more bad habits than good? Which habits would you like to eliminate and which would you like to acquire? To live the most happy and successful life possible, you can start to implement some of the habits listed in this book in your day-to-day living. The best way to start is to work on one category at a time and work your way through on the habits you want to form. Focus on unlearning one bad habit while learning a good habit to replace it. Once you've mastered your new good habits, you will soon start to notice positive changes in your life! Don't let any of your bad habits hold you back. You now know the strategies for unlearning them. Choose your habits wisely and start your journey toward a better life today!

Finally, if you discovered at least one thing that has helped you or that you think would be beneficial to someone else, be sure to take a few seconds to easily post a quick positive review. As an author, your positive feedback is desperately needed. Your highly valuable five star reviews are like a river of golden joy flowing through a sunny forest of mighty trees and beautiful flowers! *To do your good deed in making the world a better place by helping others with your valuable insight, just leave a nice review.*

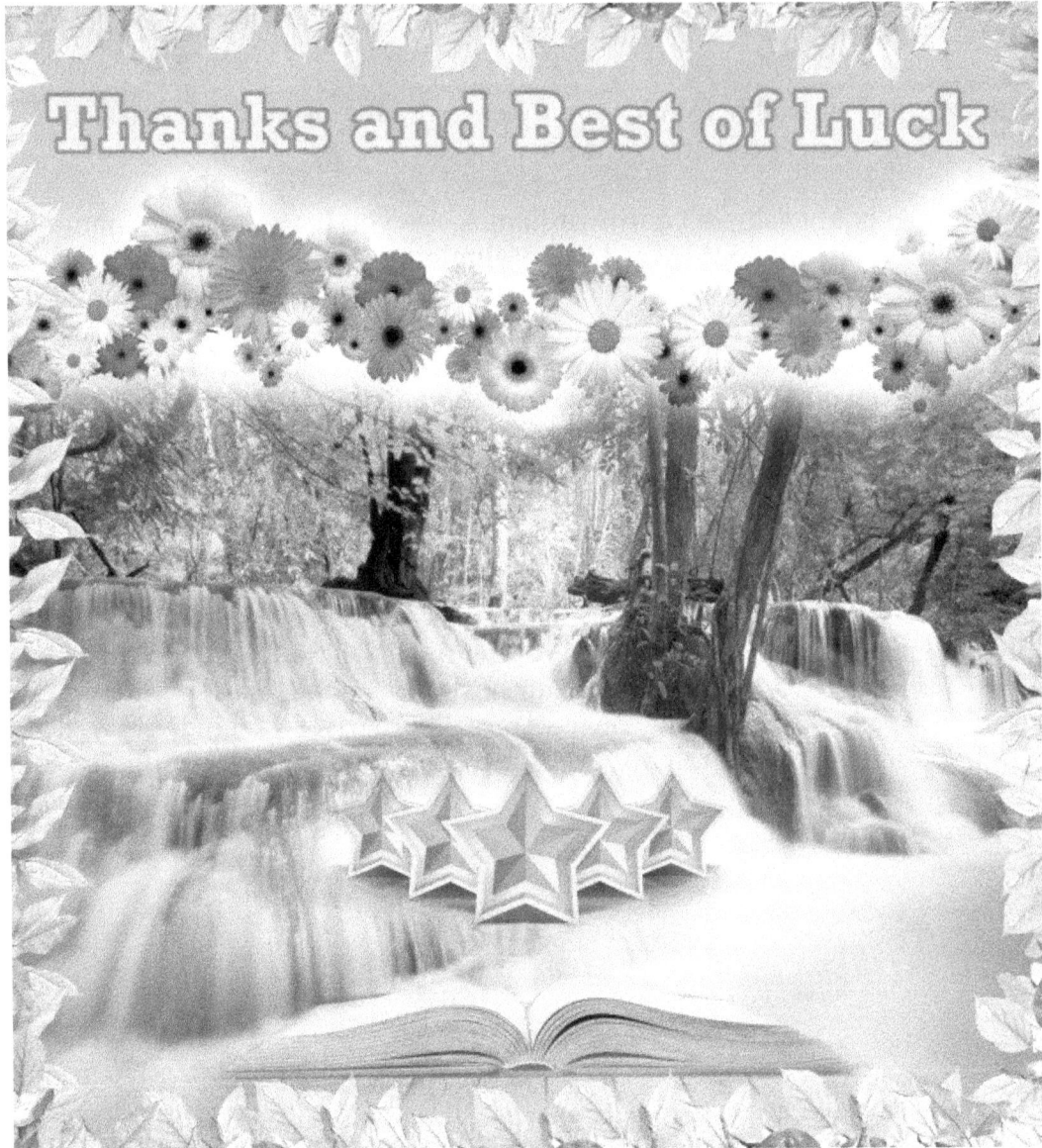

Thanks and Best of Luck

My Other Books and Audio Books
www.AcesEbooks.com

Peak Performance Books

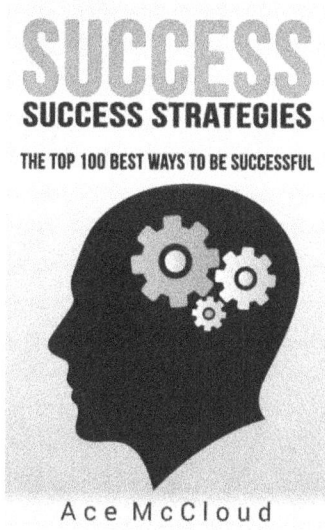

SUCCESS

SUCCESS STRATEGIES

THE TOP 100 BEST WAYS TO BE SUCCESSFUL

Ace McCloud

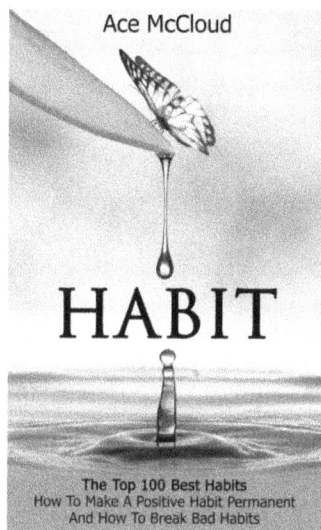

Ace McCloud

HABIT

The Top 100 Best Habits
How To Make A Positive Habit Permanent
And How To Break Bad Habits

MOTIVATION

MASTER THE POWER OF MOTIVATION
TO PROPEL YOURSELF TO SUCCESS

Ace McCloud

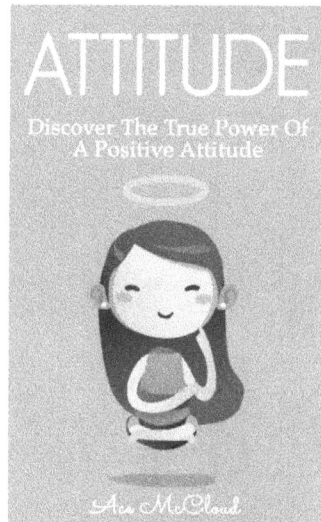

ATTITUDE

Discover The True Power Of
A Positive Attitude

Ace McCloud

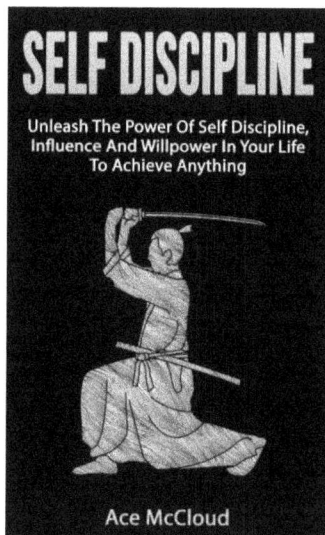

SELF DISCIPLINE

Unleash The Power Of Self Discipline,
Influence And Willpower In Your Life
To Achieve Anything

Ace McCloud

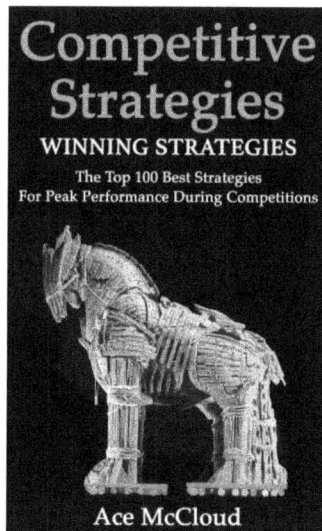

Competitive
Strategies

WINNING STRATEGIES

The Top 100 Best Strategies
For Peak Performance During Competitions

Ace McCloud

Health Books

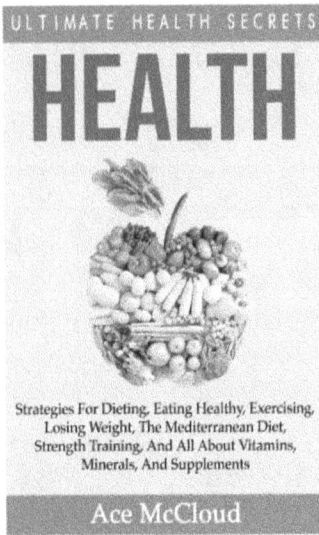

ULTIMATE HEALTH SECRETS

HEALTH

Strategies For Dieting, Eating Healthy, Exercising, Losing Weight, The Mediterranean Diet, Strength Training, And All About Vitamins, Minerals, And Supplements

Ace McCloud

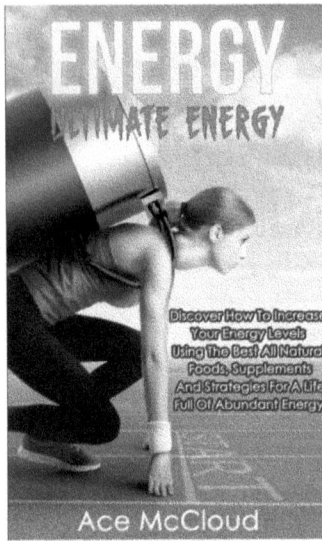

ENERGY

ULTIMATE ENERGY

Discover How To Increase Your Energy Levels Using The Best All Natural Foods, Supplements And Strategies For A Life Full Of Abundant Energy

Ace McCloud

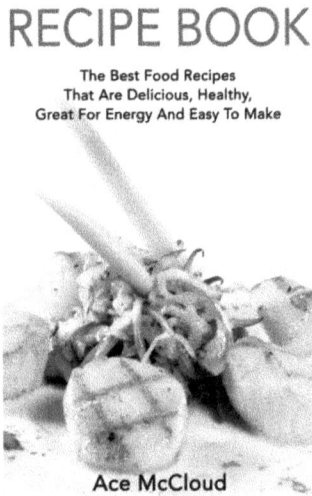

RECIPE BOOK

The Best Food Recipes That Are Delicious, Healthy, Great For Energy And Easy To Make

Ace McCloud

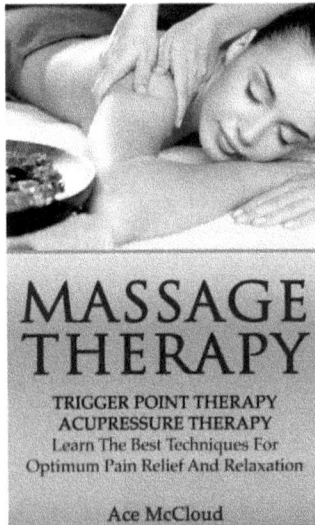

MASSAGE THERAPY

TRIGGER POINT THERAPY
ACUPRESSURE THERAPY
Learn The Best Techniques For Optimum Pain Relief And Relaxation

Ace McCloud

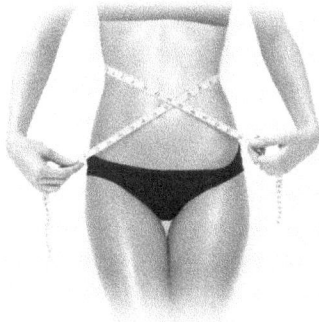

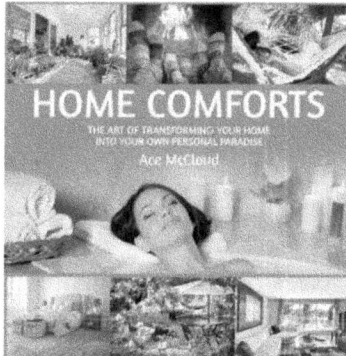

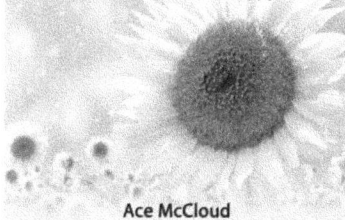

Check out my website at: **www.AcesEbooks.com** for a complete list of all of my books and high quality audio books. I enjoy bringing you the best knowledge in the world and wish you the best in using this information to make your journey through life better and more enjoyable! **Best of luck to you!**

www.ingramcontent.com/pod-product-compliance
Lightning Source LLC
Chambersburg PA
CBHW080632030426
42336CB00018B/3163